SIGNS OF Los Angeles
LOST IN THE DARK

JASON HORTON

AMERICA THROUGH TIME®
ADDING COLOR TO AMERICAN HISTORY

For Bruce

America Through Time is an imprint of Fonthill Media LLC
www.through-time.com
office@through-time.com

Published by Arcadia Publishing by arrangement with Fonthill Media LLC
For all general information, please contact Arcadia Publishing:
Telephone: 843-853-2070
Fax: 843-853-0044
E-mail: sales@arcadiapublishing.com
For customer service and orders:
Toll-Free 1-888-313-2665

www.arcadiapublishing.com

First published 2022

Copyright © Jason Horton 2022

ISBN 978-1-63499-419-4

All rights reserved. No part of this publication may be reproduced, stored in a retrieval system or transmitted in any form or by any means, electronic, mechanical, photocopying, recording or otherwise, without prior permission in writing from Fonthill Media LLC

Typeset in Trade Gothic
Printed and bound in England

Contents

About the Author   **4**

Acknowledgments   **5**

Introduction   **6**

Signs of Los Angeles   **13**

About the Author

JASON HORTON is a New York native who has lived in Los Angeles for over fifteen years. He is a writer/comedian seen on Comedy Central, TruTV, and the History Channel's *History's Greatest Mysteries*. Jason also co-hosts the podcast *Ghost Town*. He is obsessed with filming locations, historical landmarks, abandoned places, and of course, Los Angeles.

Acknowledgments

Thank you for the words:

Dante Bosco
Doug Carrion
Alexis Fleisig
Diane Franklin
Tommy Gelinas
David Goldman
Lucky Lehrer
Rebecca Leib
Jason Link
Teresa Lo
Friedia Niimura
Christopher Reece
Corrie Siegel
Nick Steinhardt

All photos by Jason Horton unless otherwise noted.

Thank you to the city of Los Angeles, Los Angeles County, and the great state of California.

Introduction

It felt like I had just submitted the manuscript for my first book, *Abandoned and Historic Los Angeles: Neon and Beyond*, when I got to work on another. Honestly, I was unsure of what a follow-up book might look like, but would've been happy with more of the same: my Los Angeles, ever-unfolding, through the lens of retroactive neon architecture and visual testimony.

Then, everything changed. Los Angeles. The country. The world. And that's where these photos begin.

On one of those first uncertain nights, I felt completely lost. Not just metaphorically, but literally, *actually* lost. As I walked through the pitch-darkness of my own neighborhood, the pale yellow glow of a local sign—the one that I had always counted on—wasn't there.

I realized that now, there was no reason for it to *be* on. As I reoriented myself that hazy Atwater night, it struck me that my neighborhood sign was one of many, a casualty of thousands of closures along countless darkened streets. It was at that moment the title of this book, *Lost in the Dark*, came to me.

I collected photos with an inexplicable urgency, I was torn. More than ever, I felt a need to frantically polish the version of Los Angeles that I put on a pedestal. At the same time, doing so felt completely frivolous and irrelevant.

Days turned into years and years turned into growing stacks of photos and essay drafts, I felt a shift in my perspective, a strange freedom. I realized that I didn't have to be accountable to any version of Los Angeles—not even the one in my head. Born from confusion and disorientation, this book gave me permission to rebuild and re-assess my relationship to the city. I hope you enjoy the complexity of this historic moment captured in LA's signs and storefronts, along with anecdotes about the city's incredible resilience from people way more interesting than myself.

As for that neighborhood sign, it's back on and brighter than ever. I'm still a little lost, but as long as I'm in Los Angeles, I'll find my way.

Jason Horton

Echo Park

Boyle Heights

Hollywood

Glendale

DTLA

Boyle Heights

Van Nuys

Atwater Village

Westlake

Mid City

Glendale

When I first flew out to Los Angeles from NYC in 1981 to shoot the teen film *The Last American Virgin*, I was put up at a high-rise Holiday Inn in Hollywood. I was nineteen, on my own, and very excited to be there. This Holiday Inn had a rooftop restaurant that overlooked the entire city, and I remember going up there in the morning to have breakfast before being driven to the set, thinking, "Wow! I'm in Hollywood! This is Hollywood!" Even though my view of Highland Boulevard was dirty and kind of grungy by day, cluttered with newsstands, souvenir shops, and a porn theater, I could ignore all that because I knew I was about to star in my first feature film. At night, after shooting all day, I would go up to my modest hotel room, look out my window, and see the glowing neon lights of the city as far as the eye could see. To me this was heaven. That Holiday Inn is no longer there, but the memory of the location I will always associate with magic. A place is only as beautiful as the memory.

Diane Franklin
Actor (*Bill & Ted's Excellent Adventure*, *The Last American Virgin*, *Better Off Dead*)

Hollywood

Hollywood

West Hollywood

Silver Lake

Hollywood

Boyle Heights

Studio City

Van Nuys

Los Feliz

I've spent the majority of my life in Los Angeles. When I say majority, I mean that other than travel, I've never moved outside a thirty-mile radius.

The line blurs between the suburban and industrial outskirts of a major metropolis, and the odd advantages that creates intrigue me. It sounds banal, but whether it's a specific part for a sprinkler, the sole repair person that works on a vintage stereo receiver, or the most convenient airport I've found in the world, it's all here.

I often "take the long way" on weekends to backyard nurseries and hole-in-the-wall restaurants to learn that not everything is in a rush or needs to save miles on my car. I'll think, "Well, I've never seen the entire stretch of Parthenia Street before…" and come across tons of interesting things once I look past the surface.

Dilapidated signage of a golden era that may not have been so golden for many… wondering how certain things stay alive or last even as long as they do.

Maybe it's like Ruscha documenting Sunset Boulevard in my modest San Fernando Valley terms.

Nick Steinhardt
Musician, Designer
(Touché Amore, Paul McCartney, Deafheaven)

Sun Valley

North Hollywood

Northridge

Burbank

Van Nuys

Van Nuys

Van Nuys

I've lived in Los Angeles for fifteen years. In that time, I have visited Chinatown only a handful of times. Currently I am a proud small business owner in the most festive destination, modeled after the Forbidden City in Beijing, in Chinatown. It is filled with history, heritage, and layers of family-run businesses. Getting to hear stories about LA Chinatown from the gift shop and restaurant owners that grew up in the plaza has been a highlight of mine. Tales of how buses would come by to take the Chinese American kids to the film studios to play "Asians" or how punk music in the '70s was not allowed to play in Hollywood venues, so they would try it out in Chinatown first. So many narratives for such a tiny tourist destination.

Why Chinatown? When I went around Los Angeles looking for a location for my dreamy stationery boutique idea, every landlord I spoke to asked, "Why stationery? Why not iPhone cases? You're a girl. Why not a hair or nail salon?" None of these guys understood the importance of a good ol' pencil and notebook. The first landlord that did was in Chinatown. He welcomed us, and so did the gift shop owners that grew up above their shops and embraced us with open arms. "We now have young entrepreneurs in the plaza!" is what they would say. I am so honored they would think of us that way. We are just women trying to inspire other creators, writers, crafters. We hope to empower young women to create a business of their own with no limitations and create a spark from the community of Chinatown.

Friedia Niimura
Artist, Business Owner (Paper Please)

Chinatown

Chinatown

Chinatown

Chinatown

Crenshaw

Highland Park

Boyle Heights

DTLA

Hawthorne

I was driving around and found myself starving and thinking, "If I could eat anything right now, what would it be?" In the blink of an eye, I'm standing in line at Pink's. I don't know why. Is it the best hot dog in the world? Probably not (although it is pretty damn good). The line is always too long and moves too slowly. I am convinced they think they are some kind of LA nightclub and keep the crowd in front to show everyone just how cool they are.

I always find myself surveying the menu to see all the great concoctions they've made up, especially the ones inspired by Hollywood, the town they're smack dab in the middle of. Like the "Lord of the Rings," a hot dog with onion rings on top, or the "Martha Stewart" dog… I have no idea what that one is all about. But being a Virgo or a creature of habit, I always end up ordering the same thing: two chili cheese dogs and a cream soda, please. Yes, everything on them.

Now, I always rush through the first one—the snap of the hot dog, the delicious chili with the tang of the mustard and bite of the onion, really quite perfect. Wash it down with a gulp of cream soda. As always, I look at the second one and wonder why I ordered it. It was bad enough to be here in the first place, as far as going out for "junk food," but there is no reason to overdo it. On the other hand, there is no way you can wait in that ridiculous line and order just one thing.

In the end, I always take a bite or two and feel that will suffice. I do love this little place. In a town that sometimes seems so surface and has its eye on what's "new," it stands out as one of those places that has been around forever. It's a great mix of tourists, chili dogs, and a classic piece of LA.

Dante Bosco
Actor, Writer, Director
(*Hook*, *The Fabulous Filipino Brothers*,
Avatar: The Last Airbender)

Hollywood

Hollywood

West LA

Atwater Village

South LA

Hollywood

Mid City

North Hollywood

Los Feliz

The vibe and history of Los Angeles is so vast and different for everyone. It can literally be the worst and best place in the world all at the same time.

The Burgundy Room was one of the first LA bars I ended up in after hours. Not knowing much about the place, the cozy and dark atmosphere felt inviting and secretive. Almost like one of those places you just don't ask questions. Still to this day I don't know anything about the place.

When I first moved to LA, I went to the beach at night, and loved that I was on a beach. I was perplexed why no one else was out enjoying the beach at night. I haven't been back since.

Jason Link
Designer, Senior Art Director (Epitaph Records)

I love Los Angeles, cracks and all. I love all her imperfections, all her bad intentions, and all her misdirections. I love Los Angeles, but I warn you, don't get fooled by the palm trees and bikinis. LA is quite capable of biting back and taking you down a dark path. She can be your worst nightmare. Don't ever let your guard down. She will send you back to Ohio penniless and straight into rehab. You gotta stay on your hustle.

I love Los Angeles for how spread out she is. I usually tell people to give it a year, and if you haven't gotten sick of her, then you're never gonna leave. Los Angeles will grow on you. I love Los Angeles for always changing and rebuilding. Like a giant movie set, Los Angeles is forever ripping things down to start over. I've seen intersections change three and four times… you gotta pay attention. I love Los Angeles because in the wintertime when you're on Washington Boulevard looking east from Venice Beach, you can still be wet from surfing in 80-degree heat and see the snow on the San Gabriel Mountains. Where else in the world can you do that? If you timed it right, you could surf in the morning, snowboard in the afternoon, and make it to Vegas by midnight. I love Los Angeles. I realize she's far from perfect, but I'm honored to call her home.

Doug Carrion
Musician (Dag Nasty, Descendents,
Field Day, Kottonmouth Kings)

DTLA

Highland Park

North Hollywood

Vernon

Hollywood

Hollywood

Westlake

DTLA

Hollywood

West Hollywood

I've been a journalist for *Hustler* magazine for almost a decade. Sometimes it amazes me; like, how did I end up writing for porn? Long story short: I moved to Los Angeles from a small town in Kansas. I had dreams of being a famous Hollywood screenwriter. And I found my *Hustler* job via Craigslist. Sometimes clichés are clichés because they're true.

I mostly work from home now, but I still remember my interview at the famous Larry Flynt building in Beverly Hills. I was a teenager in Kansas when I first saw *The People vs. Larry Flynt*, and years later, I was about to be a part of that history. That's what's so surreal about Los Angeles. Fantasies can become reality, and your dreams can die but just as easily be reborn into something you never would've imagined.

I never would've imagined this is where life would take me, but I'm loving it. Adding more to my love for clichés: Dorothy was absolutely right. I'm not in Kansas anymore.

Teresa Lo
Author, Comedian, Journalist
(*The Red Lantern Scandals,*
Hell's Game, *Hustler* Magazine)

Echo Park

Fairfax

South Pasadena

Atwater Village

DTLA

North Hollywood

Eagle Rock

Highland Park

Hollywood

DTLA

Diners in California are a special event for me. They symbolize an optimism of the beginning of car culture invented in California, and they are a great microcosm of a neighborhood. They are also an oasis of calm in a sea of craziness and bustle. They are a vanishing way to enjoy a standard meal slowly on your own time where everyone is welcome, and no one is expected to be anything other than themselves. So many of these diners are museums to an age of space-age design and terrazzo and mid-century stone work that is rarely produced anymore. You have to carefully weigh the thrill of sitting at a huge booth versus the joy of sitting at the counter on a technicolor barstool. You can be handed a fifteen-page menu with everything from lobster tail to ice cream sundaes and no one bats an eye when you order a boring grilled cheese sandwich and an endless cup of coffee… just remember to tip well.

Alexis Fleisig
Photographer, Designer, Musician
(Girls Against Boys, Soulside)

DTLA

Studio City

Eagle Rock

Fairfax

Burbank

Studio City

Miracle Mile

Vernon

Burbank

When I was a kid, if I busted a cymbal stand or my kick pedal broke, my mom would drive me to the Professional Drum Shop in Hollywood. Founded in 1959 by Bob Yeager, the Professional Drum Shop is located on Vine, near Melrose Avenue, across from the Musicians' Union. Inside, black and white photographs featuring legendary drummers, including Art Blakey, Louis Bellson, Buddy Rich, Joe Morello, Shelly Manne, Elvin Jones, Gene Krupa, Jake Hanna, Max Roach—yes, my picture is up there too—fill the walls. As the world keeps changing, this shop remains the same percussion dealer, repair center, drummers' museum, and cool hangout it has always been. No matter if you're a top-name drummer, hobbyist, or kid just learning how to play, everyone is treated the same. The great studio drummer Hal Blaine once said, "If the walls at Pro Drum could talk, we'd all go to jail!"

Lucky Lehrer
Musician (Circle Jerks, Bad Religion, Darby Crash; considered one of the greatest hardcore drummers of all time)

Hollywood

Hollywood

West Hollywood

West LA

I don't think I would choose to move to Los Angeles, but I was born in Los Angeles, and for that I am very thankful. There are these stereotypes of LA as a superficial beachy paradise fueled by the film industry, a wasteland without culture, a place without history. Beyond every constructed image of the Los Angeles of fantasy and parody, there exists a kaleidoscope of realities. Yes, there is a beach, there are over-the-top characters, and maybe a statistical jump in the likelihood of encountering a celebrity. However, this is only one slice of LA.

I deeply love Los Angeles. Los Angeles is a place made up of neighborhoods animated by a diversity of cultures and deeply affected by their history, which is often hidden in plain sight. Many people come here to find their dream, to start with a blank slate and re-envision themselves. However, Los Angeles is not a blank slate—it is a palette full of colors. Not only does Los Angeles have a past very much shaped by indigenous populations, it hosts the largest indigenous population of any city in the United States.

LA is also home to many diasporic populations, second in concentration only to the big cities of Yerevan, Armenia; San Salvador, El Salvador; Tehran, Iran; Bangkok, Thailand; Mexico City, Mexico; and Quezon City, Philippines, among others. Our city is grounded deeply in the past, present, and future. Los Angeles is a beacon of hope to so many. The city is an arts center, a place where quirky, unique projects and people can thrive. Every building, every sign tells a story and links us to the people who have made this rich cultural landscape. Los Angeles is understated, bombastic, brash, and gentle. The more you look for it, the more you discover and the less you can pin down. Most importantly, Los Angeles is home.

Corrie Siegel
Artist, Executive Director
(Museum of Neon Art)

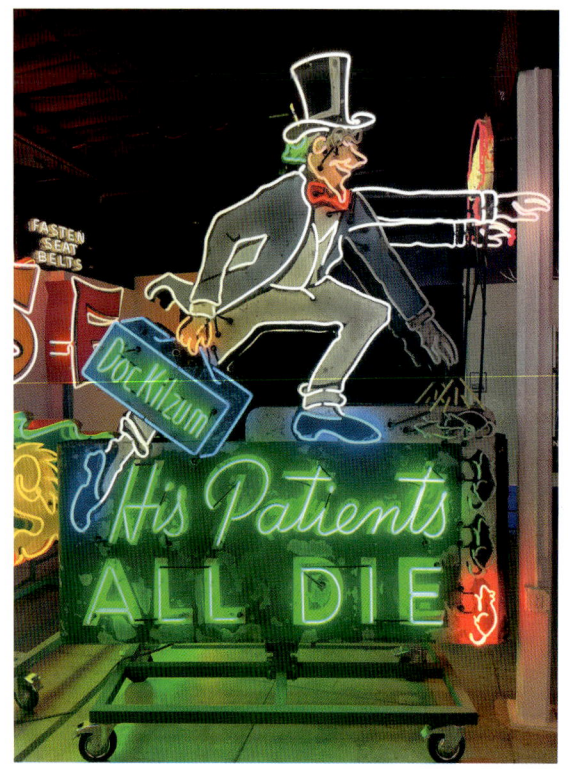

Glendale

Glendale

Eagle Rock

Atwater Village

Atwater Village

Burbank

Glendale

Atwater Village

Rampart Village

One of my fondest memories growing up in the San Fernando Valley was cruising Van Nuys Boulevard in the mid-'70s. Every Wednesday night, thousands of cars would cruise Van Nuys Boulevard from Sherman Way to Ventura Boulevard. The street was lined with hot rods, dune buggies, low riders, Harley Davidsons, and customized vans with the most amazing murals. Everything seemed to glitter and glow, and the energy was surreal. Pop culture at its finest! There were many locations to hang out at, one of them being Arby's Roast Beef on Van Nuys Boulevard, near Vanowen Street. Just about five years ago, I went on a mission to save the Arby's early '60s porcelain neon sign that lit up Van Nuys Boulevard every night for as long as I can remember. The thirty-foot sign is now safe at the Valley Relics Museum storage yard.

Tommy Gelinas
Business Owner, Curator/Founder
(Valley Relics Museum)

Van Nuys

Van Nuys

Van Nuys

Van Nuys

Van Nuys

Studio City

Hollywood

Van Nuys

Burbank

DTLA

I moved to Hollywood in 1983. Cher still drove around in a black Porsche, and rent was cheap. I was twenty-one, sanding cars at Earle Sheib paint shop in Glendale. I joined a punk rock band called Social Distortion. I moved to a rent-controlled apartment in Santa Monica and waited tables on Montana Avenue. I served dinner to Del Shannon and Mel Brooks but nutted up when George Harrison came in. The band took off, toured the world many times. Got out, started a family in a California bungalow in Long Beach, bought a run-down '50s diner in a bad part of town, because where else can a punk rock drummer own his own bar? The Pike has been open nineteen years and put my three boys through university, the first in my family to ever attend. Hollywood and Long Beach have always been good to me.

Christopher Reece
Musician, Business Owner
(Social Distortion, Pike Bar)

Sun Valley

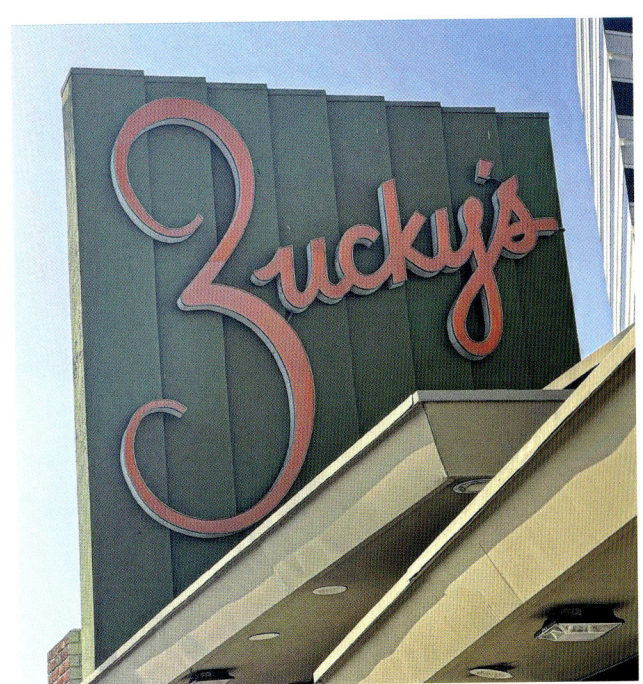

Santa Monica

Burbank

Studio City

Miracle Mile

Hollywood

West LA

Glendale

Hollywood

South LA

Glendale

West Hollywood

Los Feliz

Struggling as a comedy writer, I took a very Los Angeles job to make ends meet: I became the assistant to a celebrity psychic named "M." M was more FabFitFun than fortune teller. M chatted with me about candles and the closest Target, eventually asking me two very important questions: where was I from and what was my favorite ice cream flavor? I said Wisconsin and cookies 'n cream (the first answer was true, the second I just made up because truthfully, I didn't know and chocolate seemed boring). But M was impressed: she, too, was from Wisconsin and her favorite ice cream flavor was cookies 'n cream! As she described the assistant position, I played with my feathery, most new-age-looking Urban Outfitters jewelry on the dirty couch of her Franklin one-bedroom apartment. It was fate. She knew that. Of the many women eager to make $12/hour from the Facebook job ad she posted, I was the one.

Maybe it *was* fate, I thought.

I did all kinds of things for M, from assisting her with psychic parties in Malibu to cleaning rotted meat out of her hotpot. Meanwhile, I was trying to find a new agent and writing as much as I could. Aside from ice cream preference and home state, M and I had one thing in common: both of us wanted out of the psychic industry. Yes, M was an entertainer, a "triple threat" ready for her big LA break. I know what you're thinking… shouldn't she know when that would be? Well, that's the fun part about being a psychic: when things don't go as predicted, you can always elicit "free will," the ultimate trump card to a multi-million-dollar industry.

Free will wasn't something I had a lot of in my life. I was always working strange hours with M, and feeling perpetually lost in the hedge maze of gatekeepers to writing work and better management. At the time I was courting a manager named "C"—he had liked some of my stuff but wasn't returning my painstakingly crafted, friendly-and-approachable-but-not-lamely-so emails, and I felt particularly listless. M had me working a Christmas party for a huge production company (you know, the one that produces movies with lightsabers and spaceships) at the Los Angeles Soho House.

This party was different, though. I had been learning tarot and M gleefully informed me that I was to be the other reader working the party. I was nervous, but I had to say yes: the party paid $400 an hour and that was unbelievable to me (in more ways than one). As I sat in my booth, I started reading partygoers nervously, recognizing some celebrities in the crowd, praying they didn't want a read. On a five-minute break, I admired the view: the end of a sunset creeping over the Cahuenga Pass. The lights in the luxe hillside homes began to turn on, condemning little blinks in my direction—another Hollywood cliché, working a party.

As the evening crept on, everyone was starting to get drunk. One well-dressed attendee sat down, and I immediately froze up. It was C! I scanned his face to see if he recognized me; he did not. "What's this?" he said. I said I was giving fifteen-minute tarot reads and asked if he wanted one.

M would say that it was fate! I wondered what kinds of cards I might pull for him—the chariot? Wheel of Fortune? Knight of Swords? The "please be more responsive to young talented writers' emails and then decide to rep them" card? What could I say to maneuver in, to make myself known? Did I even want to do that here, right now? Maybe I didn't need to. He would suddenly recognize me during a dramatic tarot arc and sign me on the spot.

"I'm good," C said. He took a sip of his drink.

"Are you sure?" I asked.

C looked bored. "Yeah. I don't really think I believe in this stuff. Thanks anyway."

He slunk out of my booth and back to the bar. I never saw C again and eventually got repped elsewhere, quitting my assistant job. But before I did, M gave me a read on the house, where she said I should think about moving away from Los Angeles, maybe New York or a different city, with its own entertainment community.

I looked out of her makeup- and candle-covered window into a small courtyard. Just beyond it I could see Franklin Village and the Scientology Celebrity Center.

"I'm good," I said.

Rebecca Leib
Writer, Podcaster, Producer (Netflix's *28 Days Haunted*, Hollywood Game Night, *Ghost Town Podcast*)

Silver Lake

Highland Park

South Pasadena

South Pasadena

Mid City

Los Feliz

Highland Park

Los Feliz

Burbank

DTLA

The first time I recorded in a studio, I was a senior in high school at El Camino Real in Woodland Hills. Greg Graffin, who I met through a mutual friend, had written some songs and we had been rehearsing them with a friend of Greg's—Greg Hetson of the Circle Jerks—at Greg's house after school. They called it the Greg Greg Project. Now at the time, Greg was in Bad Religion, but these songs he had written were not punk songs. As I recall, one was rock, *a la* Todd Rundgren, who Greg loved. The second was country western, and the third was maybe like a slow Irish marching song. I remembered the studio being in Hollywood, but recently realized, after reading an interview with Greg, that it may have been Track Records in North Hollywood. In addition to a sound engineer, there was a very nice woman there named Suzy (I would learn later she was Suzy Shaw from Bomp Records).

I set up my drums in a space the size of a living room, facing a glass partition with the mixing board on the other side. They mic'd my set, and I put on a pair of headphones and began playing for the sound check. It was fantastic! The sound coming through the headphones was like something you would hear on a record, but it was me playing. For any drummer playing in a recording studio for the first time, it's a revelation. For years you only know the pedestrian sound of your drums in your room or basement or garage—vastly different from the professional drum sound on records. So that sound coming through the headphones is, in some ways, a dream come true. And I think you play better because you're so charged up—at least it was that way for me.

We worked for hours doing several takes of the songs, getting the rhythm tracks where we wanted them, Greg Graffin and Greg Hetson taking turns doing various over-dubs on different instruments, and finally Greg Graffin recording all the lead and backup vocals. Even when I wasn't playing—just sitting with the engineer, watching him work the board, taking it all in—I loved it! By the end of the night, I came home with a cassette tape with the songs. I remember playing it on my stereo and being really proud. Sometime later, I think my brother "accidentally" recorded over the songs. I would later record on Bad Religion's second LP, *Into the Unknown*. However, I never got another copy of the Greg Greg Project songs.

David Goldman
Actor, Musician
(*Fresh off the Boat*, *Blackish*, Bad Religion)

Hollywood

Hollywood

Sawtelle

West Hollywood

Echo Park

Some of my earliest memories involve my father's record collection. Every other weekend, I would go to New Jersey to visit my father and all my closest friends: The Beatles, Springsteen, Simon & Garfunkel, Jethro Tull, Queen, Neil Diamond, The Doors, and perhaps my nearest and dearest friend, Billy Joel.

I *loved* and still love Billy Joel. I wanted to *be* Billy Joel. What does this have to do with Los Angeles? Nothing. Everything. Neither. Both. Either way, we will get there.

Rock 'n roll was my religion, and I worshiped at the altar of vinyl. I read the jacket cover, inserts, lyrics, anything I could get my eyes on, like it was holy scripture. So, like many other internet-less, minimal-channel-having children of the twentieth century, I would strap on some 1970s pea soup green noise-canceling headphones. However, unlike what you might find in some nostalgia-laden TV show or film, there was no lying down staring at the ceiling contemplating my adolescence. I sat at attention. I would comb over every word and photo of any album I listened to. One that really took hold of me was The Doors' *Live at the Hollywood Bowl*.

I think I knew what Hollywood was about. That's where movie stars lived. All of them. But a Bowl? I'd never seen or been made aware of one in Bergen County, New Jersey, or anywhere in Orange County, New York. I only knew there was one in Hollywood, and it was more than enough for me.

Let's be honest: when you're young, everything is larger than life. Jim Morrison, however, was *larger* than larger than life. I think it's safe to say I was right on the money with that point of view. The Lizard King and the mighty Doors brought down the house (or, I suppose, the Bowl), listen after listen, time after time, without fail.

The reality is, as much as I loved The Doors and Jim Morrison, I didn't relate to Jim. I think I have been consistent with that fact over the years. He was cool in a way that seemed, oh, 3,000 miles away.

For me, it was Billy Joel or nothing. Other kids wanted to be Luke Skywalker, Indiana Jones, or I suppose at the time, Ronald Reagan. Not me. I wanted to be a thirty-plus-year-old Italian-American man from Long Island. Billy Joel, in a lot of ways, was a rock star. Was he a "typical" rock star? That depends. He didn't have that slick, traditional rock star vibe (well, at least based on my vast late-'70s–early-'80s experience). He looked like someone that I could be related to, and for some reason, that was important to me. I would listen to those albums, study the album jacket, and, if I was feeling particularly "rock 'n roll," pretend to play piano on the album itself.

Fast forward thirty years. I live in Los Angeles, and my girlfriend (now wife) gets me a last-minute birthday gift: a ticket to see Billy Joel at the Hollywood Bowl.

If we are being honest and real with each other, I can count maybe on two hands the times I can recall being happy. This doesn't mean those recollections are the only times I was happy. But there are very few times I can remember actually feeling that happiness in the moment.

Billy Joel live at the Hollywood Bowl—the very same Hollywood Bowl I, for some reason, felt some connection to all those years ago—was one of those times. I've been to what I believe are countless live music events of all shapes and sizes. As you probably know, when it comes to experiencing live music, there is a lot that can go right, and an equal amount that can go wrong.

This was not one of those experiences. Everything was perfect. I was fortunate to have what I consider a coveted aisle seat. The perfect strangers I sat next to were very cool, the weather was perfect, and the energy surrounding it all just felt right.

Then there was Billy. He had the keys to the city of Los Angeles as far as I was concerned. He sounded as if the collective audience had conjured him from those records. He sounded perfect. He bantered with irreverence like that cool uncle I imagined I could have been related to all those years ago.

He talked about living in Los Angeles in the early '70s, playing piano at the Excelsior Bar on Wilshire and Western, regaling those days by way of "The Piano Man." Los Angeles loved him for it. We loved him for it. I had made a thirty-plus-year journey, a connection on both coasts. My home, and home away from home.

When those doo-wop drums kicked in, and "Say Goodbye to Hollywood" was delivered like the perfect loveless love letter to Los Angeles, I was there. I wasn't just there, I was *there*.

In that moment, even though I was singing "goodbye" along with all those perfect, perfect strangers, those were just words. I have no plans to say goodbye to Hollywood or Los Angeles. In fact, I think I will stick around for a while.

Jason Horton

Hollywood

DTLA

DTLA

Los Feliz